CHLOE MIZE

PREGNANCY BRAIN

The Ultimate Guide to Pregnancy and Childbirth, Discover All the Important Knowledge About Pregnancy and Childbirth to Overcome Your Fears

Descrierea CIP a Bibliotecii Naţionale a României
CHLOE MIZE
   **PREGNANCY BRAIN. The Ultimate Guide to Pregnancy
and Childbirth, Discover All the Important Knowledge About
Pregnancy and Childbirth to Overcome Your Fears** / Chloe
Mize – Bucharest: Editura My Ebook, 2020
   ISBN

CHLOE MIZE

PREGNANCY BRAIN

The Ultimate Guide to Pregnancy and Childbirth, Discover All the Important Knowledge About Pregnancy and Childbirth to Overcome Your Fears

My Ebook Publishing House
Bucharest, 2020

CONTENTS

PREGNANCY: A BEAUTIFUL TIME

Pregnancy is the most exciting and beautiful period of woman's life. This is also one very emotional phase a woman goes through in her life time. Just imagine how amazing it is to realize that another life is growing inside you?

You are bringing a new life into this world. You are making another human being, who can talk, walk, do all the things, within you. It is something that only God can do as we were told stories when we were kids. It sure is full of anxiety and uncertainty but yet not necessary to have sleepless nights.

A mother loves her all children equally and every pregnancy is always as special to a woman may it be a first one or fourth. A mom always wants and prays for a healthy pregnancy and a healthy baby.

Pregnancy: Changes

Generally, there's no real way to tell whether a woman is pregnant especially for three months. It's a doctor's report that confirms that the woman is pregnant.

However, there are certain symptoms that can tell that a woman is expecting a baby. Certain hormonal changes take place in body when a woman is pregnant. As earlier stage symptoms, you can expect constipation, nausea, backaches and cramps when you get pregnant.

There are other changes too that tell you that you are pregnant.

A missed period is one of the most common pregnancy symptoms. In mere about a week after conception, your body undergoes hormonal changes. You start to have backaches, cramps, constipation and missed period or bleeding in less than normal are the things you can expect at the early stage of pregnancy. Your breasts become tender and nipples get darker

Pregnancy: Rest Needed

When you are pregnant, you need to rest a lot. Your body feels exhaustion and gets tired even doing nothing. This might start after one to six weeks and might not be the temporary phase. You might just feel very tired and worn out through out the pregnancy period.

Another thing is that you'd be as hungry as anything all the time. Eating is what you just can't stop. But you shouldn't control over it. You have to keep in mind that you are eating for two people at that time.

However, you should eat health and nutritious food only. You can consult with doctor about what to eat and what to avoid during your pregnancy.

During earlier days of your pregnancy, you might get very irritated and moody. Mood swings at these times might get worse than those from PMS and its all due to hormonal surges.

PREGNANCY: THINGS TO EXPECT

Women develop very sensitive sense to smell during earlier pregnancy. The worst things you won't like while being pregnant is that you'll need to urinate frequently and you tend to loss you control over controlling it. After two to ten weeks of conceiving you might also get headaches, nausea and vomiting. Vomiting whole day is pretty normal for many pregnant women even if it is termed as "morning sickness". These are all due to the hormonal change in body, due to pregnancy. Once you are sure that there's a baby inside you, you'll have to totally give up consuming any kind of alcohol and tobacco products.

It is more confirming to get a doctor's report before you jump into any conclusion. There are other home based tests also that are reliable enough to satisfy your queries. However, there are other pregnancy tests you can take for your conformity. These tests are easily available in pharmacies, stores and local clinics. There are basically two types of pregnancy tests; urine and blood pregnancy test. Both work the same way. They check for the presence of HcG and consequently for the presence of the pregnancy. HcG is a hormone called Human Chorionic Gonadotropin. This particular hormone is produced by the cells in the uterus and so is found in pregnant woman only and tends to rise as the pregnancy develops. However, these tests are not always 100% accurate. They mostly depend on the brand and also on the way it is used.

Urine test is the most popular pregnancy test and can be easily found in any store and pharmacy. It is also an easy process. Any woman with suspicion of pregnancy can buy the test kit and perform it easily in the privacy of home. However, one should very carefully read the instructions and use it very correctly. A wrong step can give a wrong result. Another method of testing is blood test. This may be performed a health clinic or the doctor's office. This is more reliable and can also show the maturity of the pregnancy.

PREGNANCY: SLEEP SOUNDLY

When you are pregnant, it is very important that you get complete rest. Try to get sound sleep and get balanced pregnancy diet. You should be physically fit to keep yourself and your baby healthy through out the pregnancy period. There are also some problems you'll face being pregnant. One of the most obvious and inevitable one is weight gain.

Normally you cannot control weight gain during pregnancy and it can lead to other problem like expansion of waistline and appearance of stretch marks. Digestive problems and constipation might even be the results of weight gain. If its only stretch marks then you can use lotions easily available in the market. They are pretty good and have been proved effective in controlling and reducing stress marks.

Other serious problems are false pregnancy and pregnancy miscarriage. You should keep close look over you blood

14

pressure and sugar level during this critical time. You should take lot of rest and get regular medical check ups to avoid high blood pressure and other ailments. You have to try to feel relaxed and might have to take medication if you cannot control your stress level.

Think positive and feel happy. Allow yourself to get the good vibes, enjoy the experience of being pregnant and mentally convince yourself that you are not getting any problems. Then you'll see all the pregnancy problems will just fly by.

EXERCISE DURING PREGNANCY:
AN OVERVIEW

Your main perspective, focus, goals should be not to lose weight while exercising during pregnancy , but to have a healthy nine months and baby, stay fit, have mental and physical control, overall positive attitude, well-being, increased flexibility, and stronger muscles, to help you cope with every step of the way a little better, every day, week and month, before, during and after your pregnancy, labor and delivery (even after and through recovery)! There are lots that can be done to prepare best/better, more, faster, for labor, delivery, and postpartum recovery.

Exercise during pregnancy can alleviate stress, symptoms, physical challenges and obstacles, associated with pregnancy, such as sciatica, fatigue, swelling, and aiding digestion. The real value of these types of regular exercise, fitness and activity priorities, even pre-natal classes uplift and inspire mothers to

16

deeply connect with themselves, be aware of their pregnant bodies, be in touch with the developing new life and baby growing inside and overall prepares expectant moms for this new journey and phase of life. There are many benefits, risks and reward, safety precautions and measures to take, types of activities to indulge and partake in to reap full promise, potential and opportunity. It is of the utmost importance that expectant moms, those who are considering getting pregnant, never over-exert yourself or put your body or baby at risk.

Consult with your doctor, physiotherapist or health care professional ensuring that any and all of the exercise routines and workouts, types of activities that you have selected or chosen from, enjoy, want to pursue, won't cause harm to you or your unborn baby.

EXERCISE DURING PREGNANCY: REWARDS AND RISKS

Endorphins are wonderful natural substances in the body that makes any workout a useful and significant experience, benefit to the body. You need to however, partake and commit to doing it regularly, as many times as 3-4 times per week.

Goals, variety, fun type activities are more likely easier to get done, if you do things that you have an affinity for, interest in and enjoy!

Stay focused and used all aspects of the different combinations, activities, hobbies, sports, routines that you are involved in, to get the best, optimal benefit from it. Working with a trainer or doing it yourself, there are many options. The choice is yours.

First and foremost if you have any underlying health conditions, issues, concerns, disease or problems, rather refrain

18

and abstain from rigorous activity that can place mom and/or baby at increased risk. That defeats the purpose and outweighs the benefits.

If you are aware of any orthopedic problems, special needs, high risk, complications type pregnancy, blood sugar issues, heart disease, breathing type illness, low or high blood pressure, you may have to consult with both your doctor and/or the fitness expert/instructor before the class or any type of activity when you are pregnant. Do not assume, make sure, verify what will be done, if it is safe, the benefits and weight the risk/reward scale, before starting a new or any regimen.

Go at your own individual, preferred and personal ability, pace and listen to the warning signs the body provides. Do not over-exert, risk, hurt or injure yourself, your abdomen or your baby. Plan your workouts and daily priorities, building the activities and routines into your everyday things you have to do. More sessions spread out throughout the day might benefit you more. 15-20 minutes at a time, twice a day, may be just what the doctor ordered and easier to stick to , than trying to get away to the gym for and hour and a half!

EXERCISE DURING PREGNANCY:
TYPES OF EXERCISES

Stick to what you know, do best and what you have evidence of will work and is safe for you, your fitness level, pregnancy etc. not putting the mom or baby at risk in any way, shape or form. Timing for/of workout sessions will vary. Find your metabolic pulse, early morning, midday, late night, then team up with someone – a fitness buddy or birthing partner that can workout alongside, spend time with and enjoy what you are doing.

Be consistent and stick to your routines, plans and activities throughout the pregnancy, early, mid or later, just adjusting and modifying what you are doing, to allow for the changes and demands that your belly places on the rest of you!

Do not deplete all your energy and listen to the warning or telltale signs that your body is giving to you. If you skip a workout for feeling tire, fatigued, not up to it, do not be too hard on yourself. Be particularly careful if you are dealing with medical issues like gestational diabetes, hypertension, multiple fetuses, have a history or an increased risk of premature labor, pre- eclampsia or heart disease. If any of these complications and challenges are present in or during pregnancy, mothers-to-be will be well advised to steer clear of any type of exercise.

EXERCISE DURING PREGNANCY:
PRECAUTIONS AND SAFETY MEASURES

According to the American College of Obstetricians and Gynecologists, here are some guidelines as to what to do and not to do when exercising while pregnant:

Stop exercising and consult a midwife or doctor if any , some or all of the following signs and symptoms manifest itself bleeding, cramping, faintness, dizziness or severe joint, lower back or abdominal pain.

Avoid laying flat on your back after sixteen weeks into your pregnancy, the growing uterus, in effect compresses a major blood vessel, restricting blood flow back to the mother's heart and to the baby.

Be sensible about what you do when, how much, intensity, duration etc. Comfortably breathing, not bating for breath, at anaerobic (or breathless) pace. You should be able, no matter what type of exercise or activity you do, to still breathe easy and talk, have a conversation with someone else without hassle or discomfort, trying to catch your breath all the time. Tone it down at that point.

EXERCISE DURING PREGNANCY: PREPARATION, WARM UPS AND MORE

Balance and loss of it are key realities to bear in minds while exercising during pregnancy and most women will rather follow advice to avoid things like avoid riding horses, motorcycles or snowmobiles for the duration of their nine month pregnancy journey. Fitness and Treatment Teams (trainer, medical professionals, Other Moms) can all have a positive role to play in this life and reproductive phase, processes and outcome.

Watch your body temperature and hydrate, do not overheat, especially in early pregnancy, first weeks, first trimester when development is at its most fragile, and the baby sensitive to extreme temperatures. Do not work out if you are feeling under the weather, are not up to it. Do not deprive your body of oxygen while working out by holding your breath, inhale and exhale normally. Remember, whatsoever you subject your body to, you are also exposing your baby to. Wear comfortable clothes, pick a safe, non-slip environment, use supports and training equipment specifically that can assist you with your shifting sense and center of gravity.

Warm up and cool down properly. Build strength, endurance and stamina at your pace and on your terms as an expectant mom. Modify and tailor workouts, types of activities to suit your needs, trimester, phase and stage, fitness-level and unique pregnancy. Swimming or walking (or alternating both), can be great, even for those who have not been exercising regularly, pre- pregnancy. Discuss with your caregiver, birth partner and such, even your doctor about creating an exercise program designed , customize and adapted for you, your needs, your goals. You could consider using a treadmill, exercise bike or swimming, to get your target heart rate up and enjoy a variety of activities to keep you going and sticking with it.

So, it does not take much to see and make a case for exercising while pregnant. It is fashionable, trendy and the in thing for mothers-to-be to do, but it is also so much more than mere Fad, Myth, Trend, Statement, personal obsession or commitment, it is a solid profitable investment in a Healthy Nine Months, with a high ROR (rate of return)!

MATERNITY WEAR: HOW TO DRESS FOR DIFFERENT STAGES OF PREGNANCY

When you first become pregnant, you may think that you will have to wear oversized, misshapen, and drab clothing. While this may have been the truth twenty or thirty years ago, these days, maternity fashions have become big business in many fashion circles. Department stores, specialty shops, consignment stores, and online venues carry more sophisticated clothing for those who are expecting.

The need for better maternity clothing evolved for several reasons:

- Many women have careers before becoming pregnant. They do not want to go from the corporate office to the nursery without looking their best.

- Many women still work while they are pregnant and need to look professional at the workplace.

- Women have more money to spend on clothing during this stage in their lives, so they want clothing that will make them look good even during their ninth month.
- Boosting self esteem in order to curb depression during pregnancy is recommended.

Whatever your reasons, you should buy clothing that is stylish, comfortable, and will expand as you do while you are pregnant.

Deciding how much maternity clothing to purchase will depend on:
- Your clothing needs
- Your budget
- Weight gain over the term of the pregnancy
- What you already have in your closet
- What feels comfortable

Women feel comfortable in different types of clothing. Many would rather wear pants, while others would rather wear skirts or dresses. You should choose clothing that will make you feel good about being pregnant.

You should also keep in mind that you will be wearing this clothing for nine months or a little longer depending on how quickly you decide to lose the excess weight. Plan on buying a few nice outfits, a few causal outfits, and undergarments that will make you feel better during the day.

Clothing that is too constrictive will not make you comfortable during your pregnancy. Looser clothing will allow you to grow and will also feel nice when it is close to your skin.

WHAT TO LOOK FOR IN MATERNITY WEAR

You will begin looking for maternity clothing around your third or fourth month of pregnancy. You may be looking sooner or later depending on when you begin to outgrow your current wardrobe. Keep in mind that you will want to buy clothing that will grow with you. This means buying items that are a little larger now, which will fit better in the coming months.

When looking for maternity clothing, you should consider the following:

- Materials
- Elastic around the waist
- Not tight fitting
- Long enough to offer coverage
- Follows some fashion trends
- Complimentary colors
- Does not appear clownish or childish

- Comfortable shoes
- Comfortable underclothes

You should be able to find quality maternity clothing at the mall, local stores, or online. The only problem you may have when shopping online is that you will have to go by sight alone. Even though there are measurement charts, you will not know how the clothing will feel on the skin. But if you have ordered from the online vendor before, you may know more about the clothing and if it will work while you are pregnant.

The key to maternity wear is comfort. As your body changes, you may find that certain materials may be more irritating than others. Being comfortable during the day will help you be able to function as normally as possible.

MATERNITY WEAR BASICS

Maternity wear basics are clothing that you can mix and match, that you can wear most days of the week, and will fit during most of you pregnancy. When looking for basics, find colors that are complimentary to your skin tone, flatter your figure, and can be worn with different accessories. This will allow you to get the most from your maternity wardrobe.

Below is a list of clothing that you should buy while pregnant. If you need more formal attire for work or for evenings out, there are many more options than ever before.

☐ Two or three pairs of dress pants

☐ Two or three pairs of casual pants

☐ One or two long dresses

☐ Four or five causal shirts (short sleeve or long sleeve)

□ Four or five blouses

□ One or two pairs of shorts if pregnant during the summer months

□ Bathing suit if pregnant during the summer months

□ Large winter coat if pregnant during the winter months

□ Undergarments

□ Nursing bra

□ Shoes that are padded and comfortable

□ Slippers/bathrobe/nightclothes

You may need to add more to this list depending on what the weather is like where you live, what you do for a living, and what you feel comfortable wearing.

You should choose natural fabrics such as cotton or silk, or a blend. This will give you room to breathe and the materials are not clingy. If your clothing is getting tighter as the months progress, then you will have to buy a few replacement pieces so that you will have enough clothing to last through your pregnancy.

When buying clothing, it is important to buy clothes that are slightly larger as you will grow into them, especially if you are only in your third or fourth month. Buying clothes that are slightly larger will also feel more comfortable when you are wearing them during the day.

Creating a temporary wardrobe does not have to be difficult as long as you know what you are looking for and are willing to search for it in different ways, either in stores, at yard sales, or online.

PRACTICAL CLOTHING VS. STYLISH CLOTHING

Depending on your job, you will have to find clothing that is appropriate for the workplace. While maternity wear has become more fashionable, you still need to find basic, practical pieces that you can wear in different social situations.

This does not mean that you cannot be stylish while you are pregnant. You will just have to redefine what stylish is. You can follow the colors of certain trends without having to wear skin tight clothing. You can wear trendy accessories without buying belts that are too tight. Taking from trends and creating a comfortable wardrobe is possible.

When choosing between different types of maternity wear, keep in mind the following:

- Do you need more causal wear or professional wear?
- How much are you willing to spend on maternity clothes?
- Do you need more tops or more bottoms?

- How much weight have you gained since becoming pregnant?

  - How much weight do you expect to gain?

  - How far along are you in your pregnancy?

  - Will you need formal wear during your pregnancy?

  - Can you find enough basic items to create a wardrobe?

These are questions you will need to ask yourself before you go shopping and while you are shopping. If you are on a limited budget, then you should just get some essential items such as dark colored pants, longer tops, and dresses that you can wear to work or on the weekend.

If you need to wear business attire to work, then you will have to spend a little more money. But you can still just buy a few pairs of slacks and long sleeve blouses to wear to work. Keep in mind that you will only need these clothes for nine months, so you don't have to spend a fortune or buy the latest trends. A classic wardrobe will work just as well.

Find maternity wear catalogs and fashion catalogs and take from both when trying to create a wardrobe. This will be fun and will also allow you to be creative with your clothing. Even if you do not love every outfit you create, the clothing is temporary.

HOW TO SAVE MONEY
ON MATERNITY WEAR

If you are a tight budget because you are saving money for your new baby, there are ways to find maternity clothing for those months when you need them. Many people want to save their money so that they can provide for their child and for themselves. You do not need to spend a fortune on maternity wear if you do not want to.

With the money you have saved on clothing, you will be able to buy supplies, decorate your baby's room, and have enough left over to add to your wardrobe is you need to later on during your pregnancy.

Below is a list of ways that you can save money:

Rummage through your closet

If you have any oversized shirts in your closet, then you will not have to buy as many for weekend wear. If you have oversized dresses or pants, these may work as well.

If this is not your first pregnancy, you may still have some maternity clothing left over from last time. Find and air out any old maternity clothing. Check to see that it is in good condition.

Raid your husband's wardrobe as well. He may have several old shirts that he does not want to wear anymore. You should be able to find a lot of casual clothing in here.

Ask friends and family for clothing

If you have any friends or family that was pregnant in last few years, ask if they have any maternity clothing they no longer need. This can save you a lot of money. Most people have clothing sitting in their closets that they would really want to get rid of. Instead of donating these items, they can give them to you.

Check out the plus size section and the men's section

Many times the plus size women's fashion section will have great deals on tops and bottoms that you could wear while pregnant. You will find more styles as well as career and active wear. If you are pregnant after the holidays, definitely check out some of the sale items.

The men's section is another great place for oversized shirts.

Visit discount outlets

If on a budget, then skip the department stores and opt for discount retail outlets instead. These stores will have new clothing that will be heavily discounted because they are last season's styles. You will be able to find all sorts of clothing for work and for the weekend.

Yard sales and used clothing stores

These are also good places to find maternity wear. While you will not have as big of a selection as in other stores, you will save a lot of money. If you need to buy a few fill in pieces to complete your wardrobe, then these are the perfect places for you.

Buy in bulk

If you are looking for items like tee-shirts, underwear, and socks, buy in bulk. This will save you money and you can always use extra tee-shirts and underwear, especially as you grow during your pregnancy.

You should also look for seasonal sales, internet sales, and more when shopping for maternity wear. Saving money is a great way to prepare yourself for your new arrival.

HIGH END RETAIL SHOPS

If you can afford to spend more money on maternity wear, there are many specialty shops that will be able to offer you more styles and materials than in other stores. While you find comfortable clothing at these stores as well, you may find more trends present. Try on all clothing before buying any. Think twice before buying:

- Clothing that has too many snaps and buttons
- Clothing that does not contain enough elastic at the waist
- Clothing that shows off too much cleavage
- Clothing in unusual colors
- Clothing that will need to be dry cleaned
- Clothing that is made of scratchy or harsh materials

Just because something is trendy does not mean that it will be comfortable. You should try to strike a balance when shopping for maternity wear.

WHEN TO SHOP FOR MATERNITY WEAR

Unfortunately, not all women can be pregnant after the holidays when the sales are at their best. But this does not mean that you will not be able to find good bargains during the rest of the year.

Look for mid-season sales at department stores and retail outlets. These sales are usually pretty good and you will be able from more available styles than after the holidays. These sales are usually used to promote a seasonal change, so be on the lookout. Also, look for smaller holiday sales. You will also find great deals at these sales as well.

Specialty shops usually run sales according to the seasons as well. Watch for signs in the windows or sign up for a company newsletter. You will receive email notification that will alert you as to when there will be a sale.

Don't forget about the internet as it can be a good place to find last minute bargains or fill in pieces that you need during your last few months of pregnancy.

Remember that during your first few months of pregnancy, you will be gaining weight, so you may need additional pieces toward the end. Spend your money wisely and make it last throughout the entire pregnancy.

BUYING UNDERGARMENTS
AND OTHER ITEMS

Underwear

Many pregnant women forget that they will also need to buy underwear, bras, and pajamas while pregnant in addition to other clothing. Underwear is a very important component to anyone's wardrobe. You should buy underwear that is comfortable under many different outfits. While you may still want to wear underwear that is fashionable, you should also consider buying some that are less attractive, but very comfortable.

When buying undergarments, you should consider the following:

- Buy cotton or silk
- Check the elastic waistline
- Buy for comfort, not style
- Buy one size bigger

As your belly begins to expand, you will notice increased pressure around your middle section. This could be that the undergarment is cutting off circulation because it is too small. Throughout your pregnancy, you may have to buy several underwear sizes as your body expands. Most women say that the most comfortable underwear is not the most flattering. Buy what feels comfortable for you.

Labor skirt

If you are self conscious and do not want people staring at you while you are in labor, you can buy a labor skirt that will keep you covered up during labor. The skirt fits underneath the belly and can be taken on and off very easily.

Nursing Bras

During your pregnancy, your breast may begin to leak every now and again. While this is normal, it can also be embarrassing. Buying a nursing bra or nursing pads will solve this problem. Nursing bras have extra padding and an opening for you to easily breastfeed, but they are also made for those who have sensitive breasts.

Bathing suits

If you will be spending your summer months as a pregnant mom-to-be, then you will need to buy a maternity bathing suit. As with any other suit, no two are alike. It is important to try on the suit before you buy it so that you can make sure that it fits properly. When looking for a bathing suit, you should:

- Make sure the suit is long enough to fit your torso

- Make sure the suit stretches enough to comfortably fit your tummy

- Buy a wrap to go with the suit for when you are not in the water

- Make sure the seams on the suit will not fall apart easily

- After trying on the suit, move around to make sure the suit stays in place

Just because you are pregnant does not mean you can't enjoy the water during the summertime. Also, if you are planning on taking water aerobics classes, you will need a swim suit. Swim suits are also great if you just want to lie out in the sun for a while. Just don't forget your sun block.

Shoes

Most people own sneakers, but what about formal shoes while you are pregnant. As you grow, you will want to switch to flats so that you do not lose your balance. When buying shoes, look for the following:

- Shoes that fit well

- Traction on the bottom of the shoes

- Made of leather for added comfortable

- Padding

- Buy slip on shoes as they will be easier to put on as you get larger

If you do not want to spend a fortune on new shoes, then you should buy extra padding so that you will be able to walk around comfortably all day without putting strain on your back, legs, or shoulders.

Clothing for travel

If you need to travel while pregnant, you should pack enough clothing to last for the entire trip. This should include one causal dress and one formal dress, shoes, slippers, and comfortable nightwear. Being away from home can cause extra stress, so bring clothing that you really enjoy wearing. This will ease the stress you are feeling by being around items that are comfortable and safe.

MATERNITY WEAR FOR THOSE WHO HAVE SPECIAL NEEDS

If you are having twins, are plus sized, or petite, you will need to buy maternity clothing that will cover you as you progress through your pregnancy.

This is one issue that will need creative answers. You may have to shop in other sections of the store or shop online to find what you need.

Twins or more

Having twins or more will be evident when you grow out of your clothing quickly during your first trimester. This may seem discouraging at first, but you will learn how to find clothing that will fit.

Begin by buying clothes that are one size bigger. As the months pass, you may have to venture into the plus size section in order to find clothing that will fit. Gaining weight during your pregnancy is normal and should be encouraged. But at the end of your pregnancy, you may not have much left to wear. Borrow clothing from friends and family. This is also a good way to cut back on clothing costs. You should also try shopping online as there are plenty of specialty stores that cater to those who are having twins.

Plus sizes

If you are plus sized, the same rules apply. Buy clothing that is one size larger than your regular size when your clothing begins to feel tight. You should keep doing this until you can no longer find clothing that fits. Shopping in the men's section may help you find shirts and other items.

You should also turn to the internet as there are specialty shops that carry many types of maternity clothing. While this may be frustrating at first, you should be able to find enough clothing to last through your pregnancy.

Petite sizes

While you may not gain as much weight as an average sized woman, finding petite maternity clothing may be a challenge. Try moving up a size when shopping for clothing that will fit. This should solve the problem.

If you are having problems finding petite clothing in larger sizes, you can also try the juniors plus sized department. They may have more variety and style than some of the other sections in the store.

How to dress after your baby is born

Once your baby is born, you will not immediately return to your pre-pregnancy weight. This will take diet, exercise, and self control. But just because you are not as thin as you used to be does not mean that you cannot dress fashionably until the weight comes off. There are a few simple ways to dress your body after giving birth.

- Wear your maternity clothes. If you lost a little weight during labor, then you may be able to wear maternity clothing from the early months of your pregnancy. Try everything to see what fits and what doesn't. You should not throw away pre-pregnancy clothing, as you may be able to wear it again.

- Do not settle for just wearing maternity or causal clothing forever. Make goals and stick to them when trying to lose weight. In the meantime, wear clothing that makes you feel confident and proud to be a parent and a woman.

- Look into nursing clothes as an alternative to maternity wear. These clothes will make nursing your baby a lot easier as they are loose fitting and comfortable. Nursing shirts are available in many different colors and styles and you can wear them with pants and skirts.

- Invest in a nursing bra as your breasts will be swollen and may not fit into your other bras.

- When looking for clothing to wear, choose darker colors because they will hide stains, and make your body appear smaller.

Shopping for maternity wear does not have to be a struggle as long as you decide on your budget, where you want to shop, and make a list of all the essential items you will need during pregnancy. Maternity clothing can be stylish and practical at the same time if you know how to put an outfit together using new clothing, used clothing, and oversized clothing.

Odds-on favorite with a best odds pregnancy diet

Gambling is a part of life. People take chances on so many things. Laying something on the line from the smallest things to the more important ones can make a big difference. Everything that surrounds us is full of uncertainties. From the time we wake –up in the morning up until the end of the day, choosing the odds and weighing them is synonymous to breathing itself. We are not sure whether going to work will be a good thing or bad. We are always in doubt if there's something wrong with the food we cook for lunch, will it make you fat or thin. Nonetheless, we take a huge leap of trust. Although, there are many odds between what we need to accomplish and our goals we take the best bet to succeed. We calculate the odds somehow making sure that it's going to work in our favor.

Expecting mothers have no immunity to taking odds. Their baby's health is on the line. Every choice she makes will lead to something that affects her unborn. It helps to have a well thought out plan to wave the odds to her favor. Pregnancy nutritional regime gives added nourishment and calories require for the development of the baby. Vital to eat right at the same time control the weight of the mother. She must be gaining healthily for the progress to take place correctly. Not to put on too much weight but not less than what it required.

To name a few these are some aspects that should play apart when planning the right diet plan:

- Daily activity
- Exercise programs or gym work outs
- Weight previous getting pregnant
- How far along is the pregnancy
- How many babies are being expected

The best odds pregnancy diet is mainly looking after a healthy weight gain during the whole process of pregnancy. Operating to eradicate any chance of a dwindling birth weight, weak immune system, undersized nervous system and nutritional deficiency birth abnormalities, that is its main aim.

Increasing the odd of having a baby that is the best bet of this diet plan. Sufficient folic acid, vitamins and calcium should be taken in healthy doses. Staying away from food and drinks that have small or no nutritional value is a good thing to remember. Increasing the best odds of pregnancy diet programs comprises the following warnings that should be abided by:

- Mercury is not good, mackerel has high levels of this

- Brain damage can be contributed to drinking alcoholic drinks while with child

- Caffeine drinks can cause the unborn's heart to palpitate

- Food that are either rare and bloody or raw should not be eaten, lots of parasite may still be inhabiting and contamination can kill the baby

The kinds of food that is taken in while pregnant affects the health of the mother and the child. If the mom is weak then she is passing it to her child as well. The protection of the unborn comes straight from the mom. When she doesn't eat healthy then the best odds diet plan might not work. Good nutrition is the best offense to sway the odds towards her favor.

EATING FOR BREASTFEEDING

During the stages of the last leg of the pregnancy, the baby actually could taste the food that the mother takes in. This is also true when you're breastfeeding. The milk your body makes is how it's going to feel on the palate.

Nursing mothers can produce around 23 to 27 ounces of milk. Increasing the intake of calories per day by 500 counts will give you amazing results. As for liquids, 3 quarts to say the least of water drinking should be encouraged. If you haven't noticed your throat feels dry all the time. This is caused by the body's utilization of the liquids in your system to produce milk. Drinking beyond 3 quarts a day is not highly advised, however. This will result to a stoppage or decrease in your milk.

To ensure that you can nurse and produce the needed milk more than 3 month rapidly boost your calories by 2500 counts or higher each day. Added calories should be taken from healthy supplements. Junk foods can offer high quantities but are useless for milk production.

Nourishment should come as the top priority for your baby. That's why it is important to choose your food carefully. What you eat id ultimately what you'll pass on to that beautiful child. High proteins are best to eat. A gram of it per pound of weight your body has is the best tool to use as measurement for your intake. For a mother weighing 120 pounds then her protein intake should be 120 grams a day.

Charging the body with calories throughout the day is good. This aids in the continuous process of milk production. The body it at work all the time, it will need all the energy from the calories you eat to sustain its function.

Foods with low nutritional value are best to stay away from. Basically, all babies are sensitive. Their immune systems have not yet been well established by their tiny bodies. Helping them get through that stage of development is easy enough. All that needs to be done is to watch what you eat. Another case of reaction of babies to bad eating habits of mothers is colic. Chocolates, candy bars and anything that's sweet cause this stomach ache. To be on the safe side, don't nibble on any of those while nursing your little one. Same advice will be prescribed by your pediatrician.

Too much oil in your diet can make your baby's stomach upset as well, same goes with too much spices. Temptation is larking around the corner, but there is a good chance that knowing what it might do to your baby can keep you away from them.

Garlic and onions tend to flavor the milk and babies don't like these flavors. This might cause them to stop drinking your milk all at once. So don't have them while nursing. Capturing the food intake of the mother takes so little to time to sip into her milk. That's why it's imperative to be vigilant. Your precious one might just be too young to love the taste to strong spices.

There is always good to know that food is not only the factor that affects the taste of your milk. What ever beverage you choose you swallow down can ultimately flavor you milk as well.

Caffeine for instance, can get your baby's heart pulsating like crazy. You wouldn't want to endanger your baby's condition. Then try not to drink coffee while nursing then. This will surely keep your baby out of harm's way. Totally abandoning this habitual drinking of caffeine can deteriorate the performance in dealing with daily tasks. It can be taken in small amounts, but not too much.

Moderation is always a good thing. Choosing to breastfeed your baby will strengthen the bond between the two of you. He or she will grow up to be a healthy child. Just keep close to your heart the best practices on how to have a healthy baby by the things you eat.

FOOD CRAVINGS DURING PREGNANCY

Feeling the need to suddenly want to munch down unusual combination of foods? What about being wide eyed about an ice cream flavor that you never thought possible to have? Then you might be in for something new, pregnancy. All the weird and unconventional combinations of menus grab your attention. Then you want to have lots of sweets and dairy products. Not your usual self, but is does feel good when you are able to indulge in those cravings. This is a natural occurrence that you shouldn't be alarmed with. They can be unpredictable yet it will pass after you're done with the first trimester of the pregnancy.

They say that it can actually be capable of telling you what gender the baby has, although no scientific proof can back it up. How? Well, simple if the cravings' tendencies are geared towards sweets then it's a girl. For the more sausage meaty and cheeses or dairy products then it's going to be a boy.

For a more scientific kind of indication cravings are actually found to be the nutrients, vitamins and minerals the unborn needs. It may be bizarre to know that a pregnant woman can crave for dirt, clay or chalk. This doesn't indicate her losing her mind. Rather one common component of those things is iron. That can be translated as the baby needs iron in its system because that particular mineral is lacking in the diet of the mother. Can your doctor right away, your might be needing supplemental medicines or whatnot to rectify this condition. When the baby's bones are forming, calcium is immediately required. That's why you love to deep your spoon into ice cream and nibble on some cheese. Salts can account for the body's need to have more sodium due to the increase in volume of the blood.

The baby and your body are communicating constantly. Their language is not like the spoken one. It manifests in different ways. It can come out as sort of weird but that's how their system works. Yet you often don't get what these cravings are really actually pointing at. We interpret most of them in a completely different manner. Take for example this, your body needs more vitamin C, all it will tell your brain is heighten the senses pointing towards the right direction. But, for instance the first sense that was triggered to show the sign is the taste buds.

And you happen to just walk pass through the grocery isle of chocolates, then the message of sweet was inaccurate. Instead of going for the ripe oranges that also tastes sweet, you went to get the chocolates instead. This message malfunction often happens and you end up have gain too much weight in the process.

The question in you mind will probably be, how to control it. Well, basic balanced diet can do wonders for your cravings. Every meal must have all the food groups so that you're not missing out on any of them. Eventually, the cravings will be lesser. It will never go away, as long as the body needs get some requirements to do its job properly. Don't bottle those cravings it, give in to it. The trick is to have everything in small portions. Try to be kind to your health as well as your child's development. Indulging your cravings is not synonymous to gobbling down pints and quarts of everything that comes to mind.

HOW TO AVOID CONSTIPATION DURING PREGNANCY

For the first trimester she is always failing to hold her food in. Vomiting is her constant activity during the day. At the middle going throughout her last trimester her problem becomes the opposite. She can't seem to get rid of her food which she ate days ago. This is what constipation does.

Alarming, at the same time, it is normal for a woman with child. Her constantly changing body goes through a new phase all thanks to a hormone called progesterone. This hormones are produced the body to decrease the movement of the muscles in the digestive tracks. This will make it work lengthy for better absorption of nutrients by the fetus. The downside to this change is constipation. Sequentially, it will create more problems like hemorrhoids if not being dealt with early on.

Circumventing the scenario is the best solution. A high fiber diet before this discomfort takes effect can eliminate it all together. Like sponges fibers take in plenty of water that softens the stool therefore making it effortless to move out of the body. To name a few there is pineapple fruit, wheat bread, cereals, oats and whole grains. So, replace the usual white bread on the table with wheat, and these small adjustments will help you throughout your pregnancy.

Prune juice can help as well, they contain loads of fibers. There are raisins, a handful while watching TV can go a long way. Target to have 25 grams and above fiber intake daily, surely this will keep a smile on the mother's face. Be sure on having them in different varieties. That way it will not be tiring of having the same old thing over and over again. Look for nutritional values on the carton labels when buying at groceries can help as well. Warning, excessive fiber leads to diarrhea that causes dehydration. Over loading the body can be harmful for the mother and her child.

Liquids can do wonders for the skin. It moisturizes the body. Think of how it can do to a constipated mother with child. They make the movement of food in the digestive system smoothly. Eight times a day, that's how frequent water should be taken in glasses. Also, even though iron is a good mineral that helps prevent anemia of the baby, it can be the source of constipation. Consulting the doctor is nothing to be afraid of.

The contents of the supplemental medicines that were prescribed may contain ample amounts to iron. Doctors are known to custom fit those vitamins and minerals according to the needs of their patient. It will be best if the doctor examines the mother to adjust her medications.

Bananas are bad for a constipating person. It has a tendency to solidify the human excreta. That's why it will be a great idea to keep your hands free of this fruit for now. There are fruits that promote good bowel movement, opt to eat those instead. Apples have the same effect like bananas.

Natural laxatives are sure ways to cure an ailing intestinal problem. But high doses of it will turn into a bigger concern. Taking in too much fiber can lead the stool to become very loose.

Therefore leading to diarrhea that can deplete the body of it's liquid. This will lower the potassium that is a life-threatening case both for the mother and the unborn.

That's why take it in just the right amount, not too much but not too little. Guarding the health of the mother will insure the safety of the child. They are almost one and the same entity now.

PRENATAL AND PREGNANCY

Vitamins are essential to soon to be mother. This is the very first thing that your doctor prescribe along with adjusting your lifestyle. In fact, the first time you decide to have children taking vitamins must be part of your daily ritual. These are prenatal vitamins. Strengthening your wellness will help you in dealing with more challenges ahead. Some studies show miscarriages are lessen in high percentages if your well equip with vitamins before conception. Being healthy early on is ideal to achieve a successful low risk pregnancy.

This may not always be true to a lot of women, taking prenatal long before pregnancy. More often than not, being with child comes as a surprise. But starting on them as soon as you know about should lay heavily in the mother's priority. Folate that is needed for cell production of the fetus is one of the main components of prenatal vitamins. It help in the proper growth and development of the baby's spinal column. Spina bifida, the incomplete progression of the neural tube is what this condition is called. Folic acid is the best defense against this.

Prenatal supplies the body those needed folic aids for the baby. If failure to take them this can present harmful consequences in the end. The majority of women who get pregnant discover their condition in a much later time. Menstrual irregularities sometimes can be misleading. They can indicate an inaccurate finding, especially women who are intermittently missing their period. This is why the best advise is to consult the doctor if there are alteration in your behavior, like morning sickness and so forth. As soon as a young lady begins to be sexually active and is at the ripe age of fertility regular check-ups are well advised.

Prenatal care should start as early as possible. The moment the good news arrives, then it should be instinctive to go get checked by the doctor.

Not every pregnant woman can afford the medications that her doctor will prescribe. The alternatives are much cheaper. Folic acids are know to be bountiful in green vegetables and oranges. Al though they offer lesser amounts of folic acid, this is a good way to help the body protect the infant's development. This can help augment the needed folate even in small amounts.

600mcg of folate is the recommended dosage to be taken. A history of birth imperfection like neural tube defects of previous children should alarm the mother to increase her folate intake by 4 milligrams everyday one month in advance before conception.

The challenge for the first trimester is how to take in the folic acids in, with the constant vomiting. Drinking a pill with an empty stomach can result to discomfort. That's why keeping the stomach settled down as soon as possible will be helpful.

Prenatal supplements are composed of different kinds of vitamins and minerals aside from folic acid needed by the mother and child's wellness. One component that is found in it is iron. This can be very good but can ultimately cause constipation. There's a good chance that during the height of the pregnancy prenatal supplements will be stopped due to the discomforts of constipation. There is no need to quit the medication, however, simply ask the doctor to modify kind of pills to be taken.

PROTECTING YOURSELF AND YOUR BABY – TEEN PREGNANCY AND HEALTH RISKS

Health Risks for the Newborn

Infants born to teenage mothers are prone to accidental injury, poisoning, complications due to prematurity, learning disabilities, brain injuries, minor severe infections, or sudden infant death syndrome (SIDS). The child usually has a weight less than the ideal and premature birth rates are prevalent among adolescent mothers.

Health Risks for the Mother

Given that an adolescent may not have fully developed her physical structure, problems in delivering the child may arise as caused by an underdeveloped pelvis. Early detection of a cephalopelvic disproportion is an indication for a scheduled cesarean birth. However this is a surgical procedure that may also put the life of the mother in danger for too much blood loss. Other complications that might be encountered by an adolescent mother upon childbirth is eclampsia, obstetric fistula or maternal death.

The absence of prenatal care and knowledge deficit with regards to psychological and physiologic changes of pregnancy results to varied complications and increases the health risks to a higher level. The teenage mothers do not know what to expect and therefore they do not know what proper behavior and precautions to make. Usually, these adolescents have poor eating habits and have no vitamin intake. They may even smoke, drink and take illegal drugs.

Statistical data of adolescent mothers who had a baby whose weight is lower than the ideal have been reported in the year 2002. 9.6% belongs in the age bracket of 15-19 years old, and 11.3% belongs in the age bracket of 15 years old alone. On the other hand, mothers who gave birth to babies weighing less than 5.5 pounds were 7.8% of the total population of women who gave birth in the same year.

In the year 2002 with regards to prenatal care, it is reported that 6.6% of mothers with ages 15- 19 years old had no prenatal
68

care and 3.6% of the total population of mothers have no record of any prenatal visits.

Other complications that a teenage mother might encounter are blood disorder such as leukemia and blood pressure that rises to an abnormally high level which could result to maternal death. And the incidence rate is higher on adolescents who are 15 years of age than on mothers with complications who belong to the age bracket of 20-24.

Within the annual report of 12 million people who are affected of sexually transmitted disease, 25% are young adolescents. When a mother with sexually transmitted disease (STD) gives birth to a child, several complications could arise such as blindness. But specifically death to the newborn and the mother may be brought about by syphilis and human immunodeficiency virus (HIV).

THE BASICS OF EATING WELL WHEN PREGNANT

Assortment is the initial ingredient to the dough. Various selections of food will allow a wide range of nutrient and vitamin intake. A diverse diet of fruits and milk in the morning, vegetables and protein at lunch time, and a light dinner will cater to the improvement of the mother's health and the growing fetus as well. Eating the same set of menu for a whole week is no fun. The taste buds will get bored of the same old dish and may even let you lose your appetite.

Balance is next on the list. Anything taken or done in moderation is good for the total being of a person and even more to a pregnant woman. A little bit of everything is good enough to fill the tummy with the needed nutrients to support the growing baby and to control the weight of the mother as well. It is important to note that kind of food taken by the mother comes from the three basic food groups namely the GO food, GROW food, and GLOW food. Go food mainly provides energy such as

70

carbohydrates, Grow food caters to the growth of cells in the body and Glow food constitute the various nutrients and vitamins. The right mixture of these three would eventually bring about a balanced diet.

Third on the row is Color. A rainbow is more appealing to look at than just the empty blue sky. A colorful plate of food would stimulate the mind to have a good sumptuous appetite. Color makes the food look tastier as it is seen on food magazines and actual plate preparations. So it is nice to note that color makes the world wonderful as it will make your appetite wonderfully great. As you prepare your food, make it as colorful as possible by putting green steamed broccoli, with succulent fish in tomato sauce and yellow baked potatoes on the side.

Weight loss is out of the picture for a pregnant woman. Contrary to that, pregnancy is the period where moderate weight gain is encouraged for the eventual growth and development of the fetus that is living inside the mother's womb. When the ideal weight gain is not achieved per month, the baby is being put at risk and so is the mother since it could result to malnutrition.

Food experimentation is common among pregnant women. It brings about new discoveries with regards to food preference. Sometimes, it even results to rejection of certain all-time favorite foods such as ice cream and the acceptance of the despicable ones like raw oysters maybe.

And in extreme cases, sometimes the pregnant mother goes into craving for some non-nutritive substances like clay and chalk. When this happens, it is advisable to suggest and offer food that are rich in iron content.

Engaging in the act of eating is a great and fun thing. It is encouraged to take time when eating by savoring each bite as you chew in the food. You allow the taste to be relished plus by trying not to swallow it all at once, heartburn is being prevented. In the case of a pregnant mother, two mouths are being fed. Eating habits should therefore be geared towards a balanced nourishment of the physiologic make-up of both the mother and the growing baby inside the womb.

WORKING FOR WEIGHT LOSS
AFTER CHILDBIRTH

Putting on some weight is normal during pregnancy. Depending on the requirement dictated by the unborn and the body itself, an expectant can increase up top 25 pounds. For others it actually is more than that. But the main premise will the body go back to its normal shape and form, will it ever?

Right after giving birth, the body still looks as though there is still a baby inside the womb. This goes on for a couple of more months until the time when the uterus shrinks down to its normal size again. The downside to this is that women are always in a hurry to drop all the extra pounds. If they fail in their quest, this leads to depression and stress.

The body will eventually loose the weight but it needs working on to get the body in shape. A little more patience is required when breast feeding the young one. Because of the necessity to take in extra calories for lactic production, the body's tendency is to hold on to extra fats for storage. This will make sure that milk in the mammary gland is full for the babies ever growing needs. A little over six months is needed or minimum of three months in order to stop eating for breastfeeding. This can only be done by those mothers who decide to give their milk to their child for only the minimum month. Breast feeding can go on for as long as there is milk in the mother's system. To be able to sustain milk production it takes 500 cal. By the time the mother stops or reduces breast feeding fat storage are automatically being reduced. This is triggered instantly thus weight starts to drop.

To get better results, helping the body by eating properly and working-out will make getting back to shape faster. Even for mother who are staying at home, exercising proves to be hard especially with the new baby around all the time. This is because, new mothers are not as active as they use to be. If they are in on strict diet the energy that they use up will make them too weak to handle the responsibilities they need to tackle throughout the whole day. Thus, in the long run, it becomes a yoyo diet effect. Also, not getting enough sleep can cause anyone to overeat. Same goes with the new moms. The metabolism of the body plunges down to a low level that burning stored fats are hard, yet as an offset of feeling tired all the time the brain is turning to food for more energy. It will be good for the body to maintain a sense of balance. To make sure that sleep is not deprived taking short power naps with the baby will help with the weariness mood. As a result, the brains will not prompt the body to take in more food than is required. Turning back to eating before the pregnancy can be taxing. But, it can be done by keeping in mind that eating has now gone down to one person. This mindset needs to be grasped by the brain by consciously making effort to chose and reduce the size of helpings when eating.

These are the realities that can be turned around with enough will power and determination. Knowing is the first step to recovery, as what they say. It is true but it needs to be backed up by a lot of love and support.

BASIC GUIDE FOR STAGES OF PREGNANCY

The guide to the different stages of pregnancy helps the new parents to be to know what to expect as the pregnancy advances and what are the changes that are taking place. This is a general outlook of what to expect. there may be a little difference as every one does not have similar symptoms. What is common to all however, is good care of the mother during the prenatal stages. The parents to be should have a good understanding with the obstetrician so that they are told by the doctor about the developments as the days advance.

The different stages of pregnancy

A full term pregnancy is normally 40 weeks. This full term is divided into trimesters which are about 13 weeks each. The progress of the fetus development is as per the trimester. During

76

the first trimester of the pregnancy the woman may not realize that she is pregnant and will not associate the feeling of nausea to this. Though this is referred to as morning sickness, it could happen at any time of the day and not necessarily in the mornings only. This feeling of nausea is because of the hormonal changes in the woman's body. These hormonal changes also bring about cravings for certain foods in pregnant women and also mood swings. All this reduces by the time it is the second trimester of the pregnancy.

The second trimester

By this time the mother to be has become used to the fetus in her womb and is not feeling as uneasy as she did in the beginning. It is during this period that the fetus has started the developing of its own organs. The mother will now start gaining weight, which though natural should not be too rapid. Sometimes if there are more than one fetus in the womb there may be a rapid weight gain, but this could also point to some problem with the health of the mother or the fetus.

The final trimester

By now all the organs of the fetus have developed completely and are fully functional too. In case the mother delivers a premature fetus during the 30th week, it will be able to survive with some assistance on the technological side. However, as this would be a premature birth the doctor's would have to take extra precautions about its health. A normal term baby would be born only after 38 or 40 weeks.

At this time the mother will feel rather uncomfortable because of the pressure of the fetus on her own internal organs and also give her a back ache. She will feel like urinating frequently and will not have proper sleep. This will make her tired and fatigued.

This is just an outline of the different stages of pregnancy, the gynecologist will be able to give a more detailed explanation to the parents to be.

THE CAUSES FOR EARLY MISCARRIAGES ARE NOT ALWAYS EASY TO DETERMINE

What causes a miscarriage is not easily recognized as sometimes this takes place even before the woman realizes that she is pregnant. However, once the woman has miscarried and the cause becomes apparent, then at least proper care can be taken during further pregnancies to prevent a re occurrence.

Some causes of miscarriages

During the first trimester of pregnancy miscarriages can happen very easily and this could be because of genetic abnormalities in the fetus or the embryo as it would be referred to in this early stage of pregnancy. The mother to be need not have done anything to bring this on, nor could anything be done to save the pregnancy at this early stage.

More than 50% of early miscarriages are due to chromosomal abnormalities or genetic reasons. However, women do not have a problem to have a normal pregnancy even after a miscarriage or two, but if there is a third miscarriage then she is termed as having recurrent miscarriages and the doctor would have to find out the reason for this and find a solution for the problem.

While some miscarriages show signs like cramps in the lower abdomen and vaginal bleeding others happen without the knowledge of the woman completely. Only an ultrasound scan can give a true picture of this.

Sometimes miscarriages can occur due to many other reasons such as:

*The mother to be under extreme stress

*If the mother to be consumes alcohol or drugs

*The age of the mother

*An abnormality of the uterine structure

*Diseases that are sexually transmitted

Though trauma and stress are not a usual cause for miscarriages in the early stage of pregnancy, it could be a possibility. Consumption of drugs and alcohol by the mother to be could bring on a miscarriage; and if the age of the mother to be is more than 35 the risk of having a miscarriage is increased.

Medical attention prior to conceiving is recommended to ensure that the woman is in perfect condition to go through a full term pregnancy it is always advisable to have a full medical check up prior to conceiving the first born child. To bring down the risk of a condition such as Spina Bifida, the mother to be should be given folic acid during a few of her menstrual cycle prior to conceiving, however she could still take folic acid if she becomes pregnant unexpectedly,

during the first trimester of the pregnancy. Taking good care of the mother to be during the early months of pregnancy is very important. Even if there is no appetite due to morning sickness, good care should be taken and an attempt to have something nourishing. Women who have had miscarriages can still have healthy babies later.

While going through the trauma of a miscarriage it is good to have moral support and time to grieve the loss and get back to normal life.

TEENAGE PREGNANCY IN AUSTRALIA

Australia was reported to have the sixth largest rate of teenage pregnancy among developed nations in 2003. As far as teenage pregnancy is concerned, Australia fell behind the United States, New Zealand, and the United Kingdom during that year. As per the data collected in the year 2004, teenage pregnancy in Australia stood at the rate of 16.3 babies per 1000 women.

Five percent of Australian babies were reported to be born to teenage girls, while legally induced abortions were the second highest reason for girls between the ages of twelve and twenty to get admitted to hospitals. Studies also revealed that teenaged girls comprised the largest segment of society to use emergency contraception methods provided by family planning clinics. Around 45 percent of high school students who led actively sexual lives forgot to use condoms regularly.

A study was conducted to determine the differences in the rate of teenage pregnancy between an economically advanced zone such as Queensland and slum areas. Teenage pregnancy among the poor was about 67.8 births per 1000 women in comparison to the 21.7 babies per 1000 women in Queensland.

Studies have also pinpointed that the factors leading to teenage pregnancy in Australia are not different from those causing teenage pregnancy in the rest of the world. To mention a few, these factors are poor self-esteem, unfavorable domestic conditions, poor financial status, and family history of teen pregnancies.

Irrespective of the cause, a teenager girl who finds herself pregnant is faced with three alternatives.

Abortion

The most common way to terminate an unwanted pregnancy in Australia is abortion. Around half the number of unwanted pregnancies are terminated with the procedure of abortion, and around 16 percent of women who go in for an abortion are teenagers.

Laws concerning abortion differ according to the regions of Australia. In Queensland, for instance, abortion is perfectly legal if the pregnancy can cause harm to the woman's mental and physical health. A woman can abort a 20-week fetus; but more than 90 percent of unwanted pregnancies are terminated by abortion when the fetus is only 12 weeks old.

Abortion, in case of a woman who has been pregnant for 12 weeks, may cost anywhere between 200 and 300 dollars. In some cases, government aid is available to poor women. The cost of abortion goes up after 12 weeks.

Put the Baby for Adoption

In a teenager is averse to the idea of abortion, she can have her baby and put it out for adoption. This option, however, is not popular among teenage girls and adult women alike.

Single parenthood is accepted now; moreover, the free availability of contraceptives and access to abortions has reduced not only teenage pregnancy but also the practice of putting out children for adoption. Only around 80 babies are adopted in Queensland every year.

Place the Baby in Foster Care

A teenage mother can also place a baby in the care of foster parents for a particular period of time till she is ready to take responsibility for the baby.

Being a single parent is now no longer a social taboo and the government offers plenty of aid to single parents, which is why more and more teenage mothers are opting to be single parents.

Counseling services are available to deal with problems related to teenage pregnancy in Australia.

TEENAGE PREGNANCY IN JAMAICA

Jamaica has the highest rate of teenage pregnancy in the Caribbean. About 108 out of 1000 babies born are those belonging to teenage mothers. Forty-five percent of Jamaican teenage girls between the ages of 15 and 24 have experienced pregnancy before their nineteenth birthday, and of these, 41 percent have had babies. About 25 percent babies in Jamaica are born to girls aged 10 to 19, and around 22 percent of girls between the ages of 15 and 19 have even had a second baby.

There are several causes for teenage pregnancy in Jamaica. The education of teenage girls is often broken up and sometimes completely ended. Studies have revealed that 36 percent of teenage girls hardly last four years in secondary school in comparison to the 50 percent of teenage girls who reach higher levels of education and never become pregnant during their teenage.

A teenaged girl who becomes a mother faces a difficult situation. Due to a low level of education, she is unable to find lucrative jobs. In addition, society and family alike disown a teenaged girl who has indulged in sexual activity, and usually, such a teenaged girl is forced to bear the burden of taking care of herself and her baby.

Teenage pregnancy in Jamaica has adverse effects on the health of both mother and child although poor health could also be due to social and economic factors. According to statistics, mortality rate is 40 percent higher for mothers below the age of 15 and 13 percent higher for women in their early twenties. Not only the teenage mother, but also her child, face great health-related risks. Research on the subject has pointed out that neo-natal death in case of babies born to teenage girls is about thrice that of babies born to adult women.

Several social and economic factors are also responsible for poor health in case of teenage mothers and their children. One of the top causes leading to poor health in case of the teenaged mother and her child is the girl's poor economic condition. In most cases, she spends all her time working to maintain her child, which means that she has to spend long hours away from her baby. In such cases, teenage mothers stop breast feeding their babies early. Instead, they start giving their children foods that don't have the nutritive value that mother's milk has. Jamaican children, therefore, grow up to be malnourished and unhealthy.

Due to her poor economic condition, the teenaged mother might have to shift her child. Shifting includes sending the child to live away from the mother, often with other members of the family. According to studies, one out of five Jamaican children do not live with their parents. Children, so shifted, often find themselves in negative, hostile atmospheres.

Jamaican society is finally realizing the truth that it is not just the teenage mother and her child who have to suffer the consequences of teenage pregnancies. The country's economy is suffering due to a labor force of unqualified and uneducated young girls. In addition, the country's resources are being used to develop welfare programs for adolescent mothers.

Teenage pregnancy in Jamaica is a complex problem that affects the entire nation, not just the teenage mothers.

HOW TO PREVENT TEENAGE PREGNANCY

Teenage pregnancy, a term used to refer to pregnancy in case of teenagers, is also called adolescent pregnancy. Various statistical studies reveal the fact that around 34 percent of girls become pregnant in their teens. In some cultures around the world, it is perfectly alright for a teenager to get married and bear children. In many countries, however, teenage pregnancy is a social issue that causes great concern.

A pregnant teenager's life changes drastically. The teenaged mothers find it extremely difficult to handle a condition for which they are neither emotionally nor financially prepared. Several programs have been developed throughout the world to help teenagers cope with this problem.

The people who prepare these programs have a variety of opinions regarding their structure and points of focus. A debate exists over whether only programs advocating abstinence from sex or those providing sex education, such as the proper use of contraceptives, should be popularized to prevent cases of teenage pregnancy.

Those who argue in favor of abstinence from sex claim that giving sex education to teenagers encourages them to lead a sexually active life. But no raise in sexual activity among teenagers who have received sex education has been recorded. Those who argue in favor of providing sex education to teenagers claim that programs advocating abstinence from sex cause teenagers to feel uncomfortable about their sexuality. They might, then, avoid discussing their sexual problems with adults.

The reasons for teenage pregnancy may be several. Social scientists are of the opinion that teenage pregnancy is due to lack of sex education. Many teenaged girls do not know anything about birth control methods. Worse still, some of them believe that certain methods such as douching with Coke or Pepsi after having sex will prevent them from getting pregnant. These are, however, just myths.

Many girls are not aware of the availability of birth control methods. For example, Depo-Provera, when injected into a woman's arms or buttocks once in three months, prevents ovulation and thereby changes the nature of the cervical mucus and prevents implantation. Norplant is a technique which includes the implantation of six tiny rubber rods under the skin. It remains effective for a period of five years. In addition, there are several other birth control methods such as condoms, emergency contraceptive pills, birth control pills, and contraceptive jelly. If a girl swallows an emergency contraceptive pill within three days of having sex, she can prevent pregnancy.

A girl who has accidentally gotten pregnant should know that she is not in a helpless condition. Even if she is too embarrassed to discuss the issue with her parents, she can seek the help of professionals like doctors or clinics such as Planned Parenthood that counsel such girls.

If a girl finds herself pregnant, she can decide to give birth to the baby and take care of it or give it for adoption or place it in the care of foster parents. Alternatively, she can also go in for an abortion.

THE EPIDEMIC OF TEENS ABORTION

The rate of abortion among teenaged girls has been going down recently. It was quite high in the seventies, but became stable in the eighties. The rate of abortions among teenaged girls has come down especially in the nineties. In 1990, about 26.5 teenagers among 1000 went in for an abortion. In 2000, only 14.5 among 1000 teenagers terminated an unwanted pregnancy by abortion.

The rate of abortion among adolescents also depends on their race. The abortion rate among black teens is more than the abortion rate among Hispanic or White teens. While the number of abortions for every 1000 White girls between the ages of 15 and 19 is 14.8, the rate for Hispanic teenage girls is 30.3 percent. The rate among Blacks is the highest with around 57.4 teens going in for an abortion per 1000 black teenaged girls aged from 15 to 19.

Age is also an important factor influencing the rate of abortion. Girls in their late teens are more likely to go in for an abortion than girls in their early teens. Out of 1000 girls aged from 15 to 17, about 14.5 get an abortion. But only 0.9 out of 1000 girls below the age of fourteen go in for an abortion. The rate of abortions among girls aged eighteen and nineteen is the highest at 37.7 every 1000 teenaged girls.

The factors driving teenagers to an abortion clinic are as diverse as those driving adult women to get an abortion. A teenaged girl usually goes in for an abortion to terminate an abrupt and unplanned pregnancy. A number of social factors also drive teenaged girls to the abortion clinic. These factors could be religious beliefs, conditions at home, and also the social stigma associated with being an unwed mother.

Many teenaged girls are of the opinion that they are not ready to handle the burden of parenthood. Some feel that an unwanted pregnancy could have an adverse effect on their social life. Many teens abort an unwanted fetus because they want to focus on their education and proceed to college. A lot of teenagers are worried about the financial troubles they might have to face if they have a baby.

Abortion is less hazardous to the life of a teenager than unexpected motherhood. The incidence of premature birth and low weight of the baby among teenage girls is high. Most teenaged girls have unhealthy eating habits, and this could create a lot of damage to the baby. The tendency of teenagers to keep their weight down during pregnancy by dieting, purging, and sometimes even skipping meals can create health problems not only to the teenaged mother, but also to her unborn baby.

In addition, teenage pregnancy and childbirth is associated with several complications and problems. In developed countries, most complications are rectified by a cesarean surgery. However, in many developing countries, teenage mothers can suffer from obstetric fistula or eclampsia. Besides, teen pregnancy is associated with a higher rate of maternal and infant mortality.

TRENDY MATERNITY CLOTHES

Fashion designers have worked hard to meet the demands of expectant mothers who want to look sophisticated and fashionable during those long months of pregnancy. Fashionable maternity clothes now form a major section in boutiques, malls, stores, and even online. If you are an expectant mother seeking a fashionable wardrobe, you have a wide range of choice ahead of you.

BellaBlu

BellaBlue leads the online maternity clothes business and prides itself on creating a wide range of designs for fashion-conscious would-be mothers. Serena Maternity, a branch of BellaBlue specializes in designing tops and dresses. BellaBlu maternity designs are known for their intriguing nature. So, if you are looking for some trendy maternity wear, remember to check out BellaBlu's designs.

Pregnant women who have a taste for the dramatic will love the whimsical designs of BellaBlue. The company aims to create designs that are not only attractive, but also comfortable. Besides, BellaBlu also offers vast selection of fashionable maternity clothes such as career wear, formal wear, swim wear, and jeans, in which can accentuate the best features of your new look. There is every chance that you could fall head over heels in love with the maternity designs of BellaBlue. BellaBlu offers something new regularly, so you will never be tired of searching through the its online stores.

BellaBlu is unique in the sense that it employs personal shoppers in place of customer service representatives. These personal shoppers assist customers to select the best sizes and styles of their favorite outfits. The practice of employing personal shoppers offers an enjoyable shopping experience for several shoppers of fashionable maternity wear.

Eva Lillian

If you are looking for great maternity designs, check out Eva Lillian too. Eva Lillian specializes in creating outfits for full-figured, petite, or tall pregnant women. Eva Lillian's exciting fashion collection includes elegant dresses as well as casual wear. It also creates designs for special occasions that will make you feel like a celebrity.

The quality of the well fitting Eva Lillian garments are considered to be the best in the industry. It offers a wide range of fashionable maternity outfits at reasonable rates. Here, you can find the latest in the fashion industry. Definitely, purchasing an Eva Lillian design gives you value for your money.

The most popular of Eva Lillian designs is the Joyce Crop maternity pant from Chiarakruza. Provided you match them with an appropriate pair of footwear and a fashionable top, you can wear these pants throughout the year. If you buy a Joyce Crop maternity pant, you are assured of a top-quality, long-lasting fashionable maternity outfit that will last you for the entire term of your pregnancy.

EARLIEST POSSIBLE SIGNS OF PREGNANCY

How can you determine pregnancy before you notice a missed period? The following methods can surely be of some help to you.

Body Temperature

Women who are trying to conceive might be familiar with the methods of noting their basal body temperature. They may, therefore, notice the subtle changes in basal body temperature when they ovulate. If the temperature remains high even when it is time for your monthly cycle, you may be sure that you are pregnant. You can learn to maintain a record of your basal body temperature with the help of over-the-counter devices.

Tender Breasts

Notice the changes in your breasts. Women usually notice a fullness in their breasts immediately after they have conceived, even before missing periods or any other sign of pregnancy. This is one of the first signs of pregnancy.

Frequent Urination

If you find yourself visiting the bathroom often, you can be sure that you are pregnant. Frequent urination is due to increased level of a hormone known as human chorionic gonadotropin or Hcg. In fact, the first step taken by your doctor to determine if you are pregnant or not is to ask you to visit the lab for a urine test, where they will test for the presence of Hcg.

However, many women are unaware of the fact that frequent urination is the result of increased hormone activity and not because of the pushing of the fetus on the urinary bladder. The developing fetus puts a pressure on the urinary bladder only when it is large enough to do so, not in the initial stages of pregnancy. Immediately after conception, the embryo no longer than an inch.

Cramps

You may experience a cramping sensation when you conceive or even during the first few weeks of pregnancy. This is because your ligaments are making way for the newcomer to grow and develop. Some women hardly feel these cramps; others complain of cramping and tightening sensation in the region of their wombs. This sensation, too, has been reported by many women as one of the first signs of pregnancy.

Missed Period

A woman who misses her period would naturally suspect pregnancy. However, a missed period need not always mean pregnancy. You can miss a period for any number of reasons. The culprit could be stress or a change in your exercise regime.

If you suspect pregnancy, purchase a home pregnancy test kit to determine the truth for yourself. Purchase the kit even if you had an unusually short period or simply spotting. The results of this test will definitely tell you whether you are pregnant or not. It is now time to put yourself under the care of a qualified medical doctor.

You might feel like celebrating after you have confirmed the fact that you are pregnant. However, remember that since you are now pregnant, you cannot indulge on smoking. In addition, you have to reduce your consumption of caffeine, eat healthy, and follow the advise of your doctor.

DETECTING EARLY SIGNS OF PREGNANCY

Is it possible to ascertain pregnancy without subjecting yourself to any pregnancy tests? Yes, you can tell that you are pregnant by making a close observation of your body. You can catch some early, subtle signs of pregnancy without having to purchase home pregnancy testing kits or visiting the doctor. So, watch out for those early pregnancy signs.

To determine if you are pregnant by watching out for early signs of pregnancy, you need to know exactly what signs to watch out for. Here is a list of early signs of pregnancy. Keep a sharp look out for these signs if you are trying to become a mother. The early signs of pregnancy are nausea, fullness in the breasts, tender nipples or breasts, fatigue, vomiting, frequent urination, headache, constipation, spotting, cramps, cravings for food, bloating, and mood swings.

Tenderness in Breasts

Several women report a fullness in their breasts during the earliest days of their pregnancy. Tender nipples and enlarged breasts are among the earliest signs of pregnancy. Two weeks after conception, a woman's breasts will feel sore, heavy, tender, and even tingly. This is because of hormonal changes in your body, a rise in the level of estrogen that prepares your body for motherhood. You might especially notice tenderness and enlargement of breasts if you are becoming pregnant for the first time.

Cramps and Spotting

Another early sign of pregnancy that could manifest even before you miss a period is cramping and spotting. The woman might experience light bleeding and a cramping sensation in her uterus a week or two after conception. This light bleeding, also referred to as implantation bleeding, is initiated when the embryo attaches itself to the wall of the uterus. It is different from the usual period because it is lighter, shorter, and spottier. Some women also experience cramps during the earliest stages of pregnancy, and these cramps might be feel just like a menstrual cramps.

Before you visit your doctor, wait till your have missed your period or taken a home pregnancy test to determine pregnancy. The above-mentioned signs are very early signs of pregnancy and can provide information about your condition even before you miss a period.

At the same time, you must remember that very early signs of pregnancy need not really mean pregnancy. They could very well mean the beginning of another monthly cycle or some physical illness. If you notice any of these signs within you and you suspect pregnancy, take a pregnancy test or wait for a missed period before you see your doctor.

CONFUSING SIGNS OF PREGNANCY

When a woman draws closer to her period, she normally feels weary and bloated. In fact, the earliest days of pregnancy, which manifest signs similar to the onset of a period, could be easily misunderstood as just another period. Since each woman and each pregnancy is not the same, the signs of early pregnancy could be different for each woman. They can be different for different pregnancies in the same woman. For example, a woman who has already had a baby need not necessarily know that she has conceived when it happens a second time. Women, therefore, should know about the earliest signs of pregnancy so that they can care for the health of their unborn child and themselves.

One of the earliest and most ignored sign of pregnancy is the simple feeling that something is not the same. It could be disregarded as wishful thinking, especially if the woman has been trying for a baby for a long time. However, many women have reported to have had this feeling just before their pregnancy was clinically confirmed. While it isn't a rule that all women have this feeling, such flashes of intuitions are not to be taken lightly if they do occur.

The earliest signs of pregnancy, as already mentioned, can be mistaken to be another period. Even the fact that the woman is visiting the bathroom often can be overlooked because this can happen even during a period. Tenderness in the breast and slight bleeding occurs even just before a period, which is why many women won't be aware of their condition until several weeks later. Sometimes, there are no signs at all, and the would-be mother won't suspect her condition until she has missed her second period.

Another sign of pregnancy is associated with the desire for sex. While some women are not interested in sex during the first trimester because it causes a lot of discomfort to them, others enjoy an increased appetite for sex. The reason is due to changes in hormonal activity within the body, which increases the flow of blood to the genitals and the breasts. Both attitudes to sex are absolutely normal, and the signs will soon disappear as the pregnancy progresses.

The earliest signs of pregnancy could easily confuse and mislead a woman. You should learn the language of your body and observe the changes in it carefully. How fast you become aware that you are pregnant depends on how keenly you can observe your body and understand its language.

DEALING WITH LIFE AFTER A MISCARRIAGE

If you have just recovered from a miscarriage, you will naturally want to know about its impacts on your body and mind. How can you deal with life after a miscarriage? What sort of emotional and physical treatment will you have to take? When will it be safe for you to try for another child? You will seek answers to such questions.

You can obtain a lot of information about dealing with life after a miscarriage from the innumerable sources that are available. These sources of information about miscarriage could be doctors, support groups, counselors, online forums, websites, friends, family members, and books.

Dealing with life immediately after miscarriage depends on the type of miscarriage you have suffered. In case you have had a missed or incomplete miscarriage, you might simply have to wait for a natural miscarriage or induce one with the help of medication or surgery. One of the common complications of pregnancy is a natural miscarriage. In case of such a miscarriage, most women get admitted into the hospital and, once they are better, go back home to recover.

If you want to find out the reasons for your miscarriage, you will have to undergo several medical tests and get yourself thoroughly examined. Besides, you should get your medical history as well as that of your partner's reviewed by a competent doctor. You may have to undergo the following tests after a miscarriage: blood test, testing your reproductive organs for infection, genetic counseling and genetic testing, biopsy of the uterine lining, ultrasounds, and x- rays of the reproductive tracts.

Do you want to try for a child again after miscarriage? You can do so. Having a miscarriage does not necessarily mean that you will never have a healthy pregnancy anymore. If you want to try for another child, talk to your doctor about when it will be safe for you to try to conceive again. Your physician will be able to give you a lot of relevant information about how you can avoid any further risk of miscarriages.

Your body will recover quickly after a miscarriage. However, you will have to take care of your emotional health. You can recover emotionally just by talking about your experience. Friends and family have to offer a lot of support to women who have suffered a miscarriage.

The best way to give vent to your emotions is to keep a diary and write your feelings in it. Participate in online forums or read books on the subjects to learn about how other women have dealt with life after a miscarriage.

Many women find great comfort in remembering the baby they have lost in a very special manner. One of the ways to remember a lost child could be to preserve ultrasound reports, organize a memorial service, or give the baby a special name.

HOW TO LOSE WEIGHT GAINED
DURING PREGNANCY

The natural processes of pregnancy and childbirth cause a lot of changes in the body of a woman. While delighted at the birth of their baby, new mothers are also distressed at the amount of weight they have gained.

Doctors say that women usually gain about 25 to 35 pounds during pregnancy. However, many women gain much more than that. Such women wonder why they haven't lost the extra pounds as they should have after childbirth. While some women are lucky enough to be able to fit into jeans a couple of weeks after giving birth to a baby, others struggle to lose the weight they have gained.

If you are one of those who are struggling to shed the extra pounds you have gained during pregnancy, remember that you are not the only one. Many women find that losing weight gained during pregnancy is quite a daunting task. Of course, it would be great if the excess weight just vanished after we have given birth to our babies, but most often, it doesn't happen that way.

Ultimately, you weight comes back to normal, but you need to put in some effort and make changes to your lifestyle.

Remember that you took full nine months to gain all that weight. Naturally, it should take around the same time to shed those excess pounds. Many women have to wait at least six months before the body starts losing the food resources it has stored. If you are planning to breastfeed your baby, your body will maintain that extra weight till you have satisfied all the nutritional needs of your baby. This is the reason why many new mothers start looking slimmer six months after they have given birth to their babies.

You need to put in some effort to shed the excess weight. You can safely lose up to one or two pounds every week. If you keep yourself busy with your work and your child, you can easily lose weight at this rate. If you find that you aren't losing weight as you should, you can go in for an exercise regime. Try mild physical activity such as walking, cycling, aerobics, or yoga. You can also visit a gym.

Women usually believe that they can eat as much as they like during pregnancy. As a result, they overeat. If you are breast feeding, you will need a lot of extra calories to enable you to produce that milk your baby requires. When you are ready to shed the weight gained during pregnancy, you have to just start watching what you eat. You could try a low-calorie, low-fat diet. You simply need to make a few changes in your diet to be what you were before you got pregnant.

If you are a very busy mother, you may find it very difficult to eat correctly. Sticking to healthy, sensible meal plans, however, will help you to lose weight as early as possible.

Printed by Libri Plureos GmbH in Hamburg,
Germany